Rattling In The Wind

Rattling In The Wind

Australian Poems for Children

Selected by Jill Heylen and Celia Jellett

Illustrated by Maire Smith

CAMBRIDGE UNIVERSITY PRESS

Cambridge

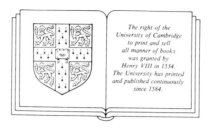

Published by the Press Syndicate of the University of Cambridge
The Pitt Building, Trumpington Street, Cambridge CB2 1RP

Edited by Jane Covernton

Publication assisted by the Literature Board of the
Australia Council, the Federal Government's arts funding
and advisory body.

Maire Smith gratefully acknowledges the collaboration of
Lisa Young on the illustration of this book.

First published 1987 by Omnibus Books, Adelaide, in association
with Penguin Books Australia Ltd
First published in the United Kingdom by Cambridge University Press, 1987
This selection © Jill Heylen and Celia Jellett 1987
Illustrations © Maire Smith 1987
Typeset by Caxtons Pty Ltd, Adelaide
Printed in Hong Kong

ISBN 0 521 35160 X

Contents

Short Song

Here's my song,
It's quite a whizz—
Not too long:
That's all there is!

Peter Wesley-Smith

I

A place I like is the garage roof
Where the loquat leaves
All shiny and green
All polished and varnished
Make a shady screen
From grown-up eyes.

Our secret ship is the garage roof
Where the loquat leaves
Are the flags and sail
And the chicken coop
Is a great blue whale
With turquoise eyes.

Catherine Warry

Plumpoem

Flicking plumstones out of the tree
to pester the dogs in the shade
then back to fill the creaking basket—

plumjuice spikes the saliva I crush
on the roof of my mouth. Always
a thousand wasps rev wildly or whimper or doze.

Motes of sunlight move in flakes
through the shining leaves
on to the duskblooming flanks of plums

& my fingers enter that light—
orange and magnificent rose
in every pore & every flickering joint,

every soft line of myself
as I take the purple flesh of the plums—
blotching brighter where my fingers touch—

sometimes there's a birdpeck, or leafhooded maggothole,
sometimes a wineskin rotten with brown booze
or just a thin lantern bright with yellow wasps—

but there are so many more
& the lode of the sun has still more time
soaking the afternoon outside the leaves

with our beauty. It is good
to be alive & taste all summer over
that bright plumjuice.

Norman Talbot

On the Spot

To the memory of Charles Buckmaster

ripe oranges
squirting
light
stain
your
mouth

next
summer
the pips
found
in
your
pocket

hold
part
of
that
sun

Robert C. Boyce

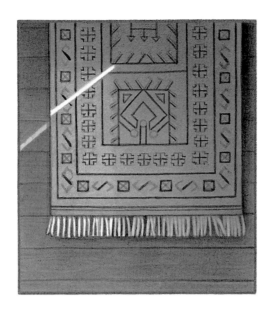

Sunstruck

There's a pencil of light
On my bedroom rug;
It lies there so bright
I nearly picked it up.
When I put my finger on it
It warmed me to the bone.
I'd like to write with it
A letter of pure sunshine
But I've got to go to school now
And it won't be there when I
come home.

Darien Smith

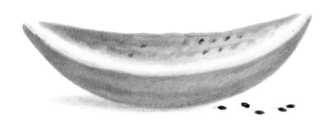

Watermelons

Self-sown

in the sandy down-slip
from the ice works
they grew
where discarded
lumps of broken ice
would spill and thaw
into the rutted dirt
of cart and waggon track

swell to green cold globes
fed to the donkeys

striped drums
of pink chilled juice
we carried after school
to cool dark ditches

dripping chins

green rind ear-to-ear.

Jeff Guess

Macartney's Cow

Returning, tadpole-laden, from the creek,
we often watched Macartney's brindle cow
stolidly commune with grass.
Stirred one day by last week's Western
we rode the cow, all four of us,
clambering up her placid sides
till, perched upon her bony back,
we dug in the spurs
and cracked imaginary whips.
Calmly our steed subsided to her knees,
rolled to one side, rubbed us in the dirt,
resumed her feet and slowly walked away,
her affronted dignity reproving
both John Wayne and dreaming boys.

Michael Dugan

From **Growing Up Alone**

At Cheerio Point me and Sandy
knew a place where

we'd go behind the tree sometimes
and stare into the eyes of God

they were in the face
of an old yellow cat who'd gone mad

once we had looked
we wouldn't be able to move

sometimes we'd have to sit there
for hours waiting

before it let us go

Robert Adamson

Bamboo Tiger

Bamboo grew
in the creek bed,
tall sticks
rattling in the wind.
Close, dark thickets
where tigers hid,
growling softly
as they waited to pounce.
Tiptoeing past
I would hear them,
see their round eyes
glaring from shadows.
And I would run and run,
faster than wind
across the fields.
Faster than tigers,
who returned to their thicket,
jaws slavering, outwitted again.

Michael Dugan

all day sucker

i am sitting up in a tree
not that i am given to climbing trees
i am not
i am not given either to
bird watching
bird nesting
or birdy talk
i do not become excited at the sight
of a snowy tufted puffingchook
a mottled goosefinch
a rare hebridean cat-thrush
a green billed fingertit
an early auk
a yellow owl
and look o look daddy
the african puddingbird
chirrup chirrup chirrup
tweeeeeet tweet
tuwhit tuwho
ernie mcwhidden belongs to the
feathered friends league
and that's how he goes on
but i don't
i am sitting up in a tree
because
it's the best place to eat an all day sucker
if you don't want
to share it
with anyone

Redmond Phillips

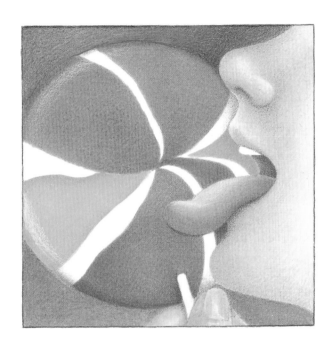

the school lunch poem

mum says she tries to put variety
into my school lunch
but i don't see how she can
when i unwrap ham sandwiches
three days in a row

mum also says if i don't like the way
she does it
i can always make it myself

Jenny Boult

where are you going?

i've put my bus pass in my pocket & packed my bag
my shoelaces are neatly tied
i've made my own lunch, by myself
won't mum be surprised?

i've brushed my hair & teeth
looked in the mirror to see i'm o.k.
i've done my homework, i'm not running late
i'm ready to go now.
bye mum.

"where are you going?
it's saturday."

Jenny Boult

Kim's Collection

Kim collects all kinds of things:
lolly sticks and can-top rings,
    coloured straws,
    jagged stones,
    plastic cartons,
    old white bones.
When the beach has jetsam there
Kim will fossick everywhere:
    soggy seaweed,
    (salty smells),
    tattered feathers,
    broken shells,
Bits of cork and empty tins,
dry sea-urchins, fishes' fins,
    chunks of charcoal
    from some fire,
    lengths of string
    and tangled wire;
Marble pebbles, smoothed by ocean,
screw-top lids from sun-tan lotion,
    half a twisting
    birthday candle,
    old false teeth,
    a battered sandal.
Some folk scorn the weird selection
of the things in this collection;
    others love
    to touch and see them,
    find such fun
    in Kim's museum.

David Bateson

Tide Talk

The tide and I had stopped to chat
About the waves where seabirds sat,
About the yachts with bobbing sails
And quite enormous, spouting whales.

The tide has lots to talk about.
Sometimes it's in. Sometimes it's out.
For something you must understand,
It's up and down across the sand;
Sometimes it's low and sometimes high.
It's very wet and never dry.

The tide, quite crossly, said: "The sea
Is always out there pushing me.
And just when I am feeling slack,
It sends me in then drags me back.
It never seems to let me go.
I rise. I fall. I'm to and fro."

I told the tide, "I know it's true
For I am pushed around like you.
And really do they think it's fair?
Do this. Do that. Come here. Go there."

Then loudly came my parents' shout.

So I went in.

The tide went out.

Max Fatchen

The Back Step

Every day at sunset
We watch the cows go by.
We always like to be there,
My grandmother and I.

They always go to water
Along the same old track,
But some must have a wander
And some go quickly back.

There's Mabel, Maude and Judy,
Mitzi who's always late
And Betsy Anne, who's rubbing
Her flanks against the gate.

Not for them the drabness
Of car or bike or train.
For them it's warming sunshine
And clear, refreshing rain.

It's giving milk each morning
And dozing in the grass.
It's never thinking over
How each new day will pass.

And we can share a little
In all this peace around,
Sitting on the back step
Scratching on the ground.

And so we dream together
And watch the cows go by,
While shelling peas and chatting—
My grandmother and I.

Lee Knowles

Down and Up

Words	top.
are	very
nice	the
to	reach
speak	you
and	until
read	stop
and	never
some	and
are	along
very	read
long	so
indeed	play
and	to
if	out
you	come
are	us
the	like
reading	words
age	for
you'll	way
reach	different
the	a
bottom	quite
of	going
this	we're
page. Now read across.	We'd like to say

Max Fatchen

Sea Hunt

Up again, down again,
Down to the beach again,
Go diving and diving,
Searching for seaweed.

Down again, up again,
Down to the beach again,
Go swimming and swimming,
Diving for pearls.

Evangeline Yaruso

i can read upside down

upside down
everything looks much the same
only more different
your hair comes out of your head
like a flame
a long tongue of hair
licking the ground
and the grass falls out of the earth
and the trees drop down and brush the sky
and church spires balance on
horizons
like the tricks seals do in circuses
and smoke wriggles down out of chimneys
like a worm coming out of a drain pipe
and birds fly upside down like our gallant airmen
with the earth whirling overhead
faster and faster and faster
then slower
then bells ring
and the sea roars in one's ears
and you feel sick in the stomach

i can read upside down
but it's easier if you sit in the normal position
and hold the book upside down
then you don't feel sick or anything
and you only have to read backwards like
i can read upside down

Redmond Phillips

II

The Sea

Deep glass-green seas
chew rocks
with their green-glass jaws.
But little waves
creep in
and nibble softly at the sand.

Lilith Norman

Limpets

Down there on the dark rock sharp to the foot,
browsing on greenstuff as the cattle do,
the limpets,
whose houses are little pyramids of stone.

Deep in the press of the tide in the dim light
where the to-fro drag of the waves moves the
    weed-fronds
whose tips describe their endless sensuous curves,
very like tanks and other armoured machines,
the limpets deploy.

Now who would ever believe,
seeing these creatures when the water is gone,
clamped fast, fixed rigid,
or cementing themselves at a touch,
they lift their skirts and dance a slow pavan
when the cold green water replaces the hostile
    sun?

                            William Hart-Smith

Gold Fish

On the shining surface of the sea
So calm and smooth
The moon shines.

There in the reef
Swim the gold fish
Through the beautiful corals.

The moon comes out from a cloud.
"Swim up, swim up, little fish,
For my brilliant lights are wasted
On the smooth calm surface."

Now the eels crawl out,
The crabs wake up,
And living things rub their faces
To see the gold fish talking to the moon.

                                    Edith Mary Jinga

Prawning

In the nine o'clock dark we wait for moon-rise
Over the prussian blue lake
That looks like ink
Not water.
Our cold feet walk with a faint
Watery slap
The perimeter of the empty baths
And we mutter about not enough hands
For nets and buckets and swaying lantern.
Watching.
Waiting.
Watching.
The lantern-light draws a perfect circle in the lake
That reveals
A world of palest green
All one colour and shimmering
The sand, the weed, and swaying water.
And held there
Just for an instant
A prawn.
A mere outline
Green as the water.
As we reach for the net
A twitch and it's gone.

Catherine Warry

Lake

I can't hold it, keep it.
It's full of mountains fluttering down,
And trees—or rather their other selves.

I can break it with a stone,
My foot; and I can almost see
Just what it's thinking.   I'm certain it's thinking.

A fisherman unpacks himself gently
On a ledge, and soon his line
Is holding the lake exactly.

R. A. Simpson

Seashell

*Translated from the Spanish
of Federico Garcia Lorca*

They've brought me a seashell.

Inside it sings
a map of the sea.
My heart
fills up with water,
with smallish fish
of shade and silver.

They've brought me a seashell.

K. F. Pearson

Snail

The snail on the pane
Makes the glass sing and miles away
A train rings the rails.

Above the cutting
Smoke blows through the trees.
Woo! Hoo!

Over glass and hill
The snail draws its carriage
Leaving a silver trail.

David Campbell

Song: The Railway Train

Translated by G. Taplin

You see the smoke at Kapunda
The steam puffs regularly,
Showing quickly, it looks like frost,
It runs like running water,
It blows like a spouting whale.

Aboriginal: Narranyeri

Continent and Island

Our island is holy,
Being even as it came from Creator.
It is lovely, beyond
Any singing of it,
Watched by its hills
Grand and beautiful
Running gradually into the sea.

John Trevor Kason

A Wind from the Sea

Wind that breaks across the bay
tumbles the grass in green and grey.

Lapped by grass, with posts alean,
the house patchpeels in grey and green.

High up in those blistered walls
a window lifts, some dimness falls.

Loosed into the weather, grey
tatters of lacework suck and splay.

Past those curtains lies a room.
Almond husks bear such grey bloom.

In that room some figure stands:
brushing a greyness from its hands.

Holding back the bellying lace.
Wind, salt wind, across its face.

Randolph Stow

Children Lost

On a lonely beach the old wreck lies
With its rusted ribs and sides,
To the biting lash of the salty wind
And the drive of the flooding tides.

Years ago it was wrecked, they said,
Wrecked where the loud winds blew.
All hands were lost in the sad affair
And the women and children too.

It's there I went on a moonlit night
Where the cliffs slope wild and steep,
And suddenly came a shout and cry
As the ship awoke from sleep.

She had her masts and sails again,
No longer a broken wreck
While the sailors sang as they hauled the ropes
And the children played on the deck.

They shouted and played on the heaving deck
Or sat at their cabin tea
While the sly winds filled the swelling sails
On the toss of the cunning sea.

But no one knew and no one dreamed . . .
Beware of the sailor's boast
That says he's master of the sea
Or king of the rugged coast.

For I heard it all on a moonlit night,
The eager waves' wild roar
And the cries of the crew as the great sea threw
That broken ship ashore.

Where, where the children? Never a sound
On the reef's cold rock and stone
For the selfish sea had taken them all
And kept them for its own.

"Perhaps, perhaps . . .," the sea kings said
To the children deep and drowned,
"We will let you go to the shore again
But by this bond you're bound.

"That you are the children of the sea,
Of the waves and the dolphin's track
On a moonlit night we'll set you free
But then we'll call you back . . .

"On the ghostly beach you will play your games
But far from the cheerful town
Then back we'll call you, children, back
When the cold-eyed moon goes down."

Or so it seemed to come to me
In the voice of the wind and the tide
As I stood on the beach where the moonlight fell
On the ship with the broken side.

And did I hear and could I hear
The sound of some voices there?
Did figures form and vanish again
In the strange and haunted air?

How shall I tell you what I felt
And how will you understand
What, by the moon, my own eyes saw—
Small footprints in the sand!

Max Fatchen

III

bird hits boy

I like rain
I like puddles
I like mess
I like muddles

dad drives a grader
that mum employs
to drive a path-way
through my toys

I go hang-gliding
on my trike
pedalling, pedalling
and flying my kite

night is a freeway
to th moon
past magpie geese
honk my balloon

use th sun
for a parachute
float softly down
toot toot toot

look out birds
look out jet
bird never heard
land in bed

no one knows
how I tell weather
on my pillow
just one feather

Eric Beach

Genius Loci

The Spirit of the Place

When I can't sleep and prove
a pain in the neck to myself
I will sneak downstairs, dress up warmly
and squeeze into whelming darkness
or piccaninny daylight, where
I may just glimpse at a corner
one of the Jika Jika slipping away
lapped in a possumskin rug.

I will hurry like steam to the corner,
ever so much wanting to say,
"Hey, wait. I have so much that I . . ."
But there will only be
broad street, creamy houses, dew
and a silence of black shrubs.

Maybe if I got up
a little more smartly next time,
got out on the road quick,
I could sneak up closer
on that dark tribesman in his furry cloak
and ask him . . .
        oh, something really deep:

something off the planet.

Chris Wallace-Crabbe

Milking Song

Like a sandstone sculpture, the ginger cat
Sits on his tipsy plinth of fence,
Snug in the arc of his tidy tail
And feigning a fine indifference
To morning's leisured blossoming,
The hills' slow stirring to unfold
The hour's intrinsic loveliness,
The curve of sky, the spill of gold.

Spun galaxies of mislaid stars,
The yellow thornbills prank the air,
Conspiring to confuse the sun;
And down the hill my lady-mare,
A wagtail at her wither, comes;
And magpies fill the sky with song
And hang the trees with leafy notes
For flocks of winds to flute among.

The soft froth lips the bucket's rim;
The red cow roughs her tongue around
The empty feed-bin's edge . . . The cat,
Suddenly vital at the sound,
Leaps in a golden arc from fence
To ground and then, with flanks grown thin
And eyes gone green, he laps at last
His nectar from a rusty tin.

                                    Anne Bell

45

Cow Cocky

for John Thomas Gregson, 1905–1986

"When I was a boy,"
he said.
"I'd be milkin' the cows
an hour before the sun got up.
With me feet bare, I'd go out into the paddock,
with the frost crunching underfoot,"
he said.
"And two cows were in the holding yard
wondering when they'd be fed.
But there'd be no feed today,"
he said.
"Today Dad would bring his mate, Bert, over
and slaughter those two cows,"
he said.
"It was all over
before the mist could rise,"
he said.

Samuel Wardleworth

Baggin'

"G'up t' th' 'ouse 'n' get Baggin'.
'N' put wood in th' 'ole as y' go."
Well, not knowing what he said,
but not keen to be seen as daft
on my first job, I left him
crouched under cows' udders,
and shut the milk shed door.

Stepping round the frosty yard,
slapping my arms against the chill,
I saw his wife at her window sill
in the vapours of a can of tea
and plates of melted-butter toast:
"Quick wi' thee, Lad," she scolded,
"'N' get this Baggin' out o' cold!"

So, as if I'd known all along,
I received the steaming load,
then, swollen with duty, strode
down the yard to the feed-room,
where bales of hay and straw
were set, and men who'd worked
all morning sat, growling
"Baggin's 'ere. 'Bout time too!"

John Wright

Morning

Feeding chickens, pollard scattered like wet sand.

—Jump down stolidly from their roost
as an old sailor jumps
with his peg-leg;
underneath half a corrugated iron tank,
open ended.

I'm stepping around the bare black ground;
wire-netting propped
with lopped poles.
Moss about, bits
of brick poking through and
bones. Rusted wrench
pressed into the ground, jaws open:
a tyrannosaurus head. Reeds.

In packing cases, one side gone, the eggs
in dry grass;
on this cold morning, they're warm, smooth:
Surprising stone

almost weightless.
Bent over;
at the side of my face
the silver, liquid paddocks; steam.
My eyes and nose are damp, I see through my own smoke.

Finding the eggs, dry—the colour of dry sand.

Robert Gray

48

Fanfare

Feed time
it's all downhill to the duckhouse
like a sampan on the dam.
Ducks scurry
webfoot hotfoot uphill
quack that they're hungry.
Cacophony,
four appleyards two bitsers
one remaining khaki campbell.
Only seven. The fox again.
We ease the mooring rope the duckhouse
to the edge.
Feed spills to the feeder.
Good fat ducks. Handsome plumage,
flash of jade to agate, bronze to turquoise
snake-necked they gobble and gaggle.
Gullet of meal dibble of water
splat to the duckboard and away again.
Flotilla of seven afloat
quack to tail
mirror the evening.
Serene their trail on silver water.

Adèle Kipping

parrots
with vermilion bands and beak
green-iris camouflaging
are acrobats
swinging on trapezes of green gum leaves
tips

they carry their very own safety net
their green-yellow tail feathers
which spray out like palm fronds
parachuting

Neil Paech

I'm sitting inside

I'm sitting inside
from the door. A shirt of mine's
hung on the line
in the rain.

And that rain keeps on
steadily
drifting. I can see it
against the dark
tree trunk,
like a movie screen
flicker.

And in the rain
a bedsheet
is also pegged
up, unevenly, along that
sagging
line.

It's there,
patient
and heavy as
a rhinoceros
in whitewash.

Robert Gray

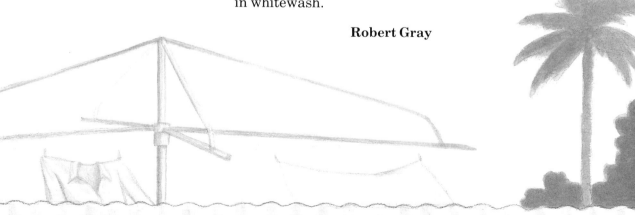

Frogs

for Elizabeth Scott

Fat frogs squat greenly
in waterholes.
Swim with hind legs
on hinges.

They sleep all day
under tankstands
where damp fern fronds
hang in fringes.

But on blowy nights
when rain rattles
on the stiff leaves
of palm and mango,

they swell their throats,
bellow, honk and tinkle—
that's what I call
a frog fandango.

Bill Scott

Night Herons

It was after a day's rain:
the street facing the west
·was lit with growing yellow;
the black road gleamed.

First one child looked and saw
and told another.
Face after face, the windows
flowered with eyes.

It was like a long fuse lighted,
the news travelling.
No one called out loudly;
everyone said "Hush".

The light deepened; the wet road
answered in daffodil colours,
and down its centre
walked the two tall herons.

Stranger than wild birds, even,
what happened on those faces:
suddenly believing in something,
they smiled and opened.

Children thought of fountains,
circuses, swans feeding:
women remembered words
spoken when they were young.

Everyone said "Hush";
no one spoke loudly;
but suddenly the herons
rose and were gone. The light faded.

Judith Wright

Back Steps Lookout

A cross-framed square of kitchen light
outlines the tomato bed.
A silhouette of my head boats the shallows
of one particular
frilled and spiky pumpkin leaf.

The dark behind the brief dark
that I can see
is very deep.
Footpads with no feet stop, then pass;
the leaves get up and walk.
The mangoes stalk with crabs' eyes through their tree.
In a wet temper night skates about the grass
like a maniac in a black
rectangular overcoat.

Rhyll McMaster

Horses

for Alison

We had an old stables in the backyard
under the chopped Weeping Fig.
If you peeked inside the narrow door you would see
that hay rack
the chaff troughs—
there were rusty rings for tethering
but
where were the horses?

We dreamed of horses in those stables
stamping hooves, snorting
stamping against the floor
raising their tails
we dreamed their hot breathing
the shovel loads of manure
in our cobwebbed stables.

Our stables look deprived but friendly.
We live in a suburb. There could be no
exercise, certainly not for big sweating fly
attracting smell-of-confinement-and-paddock-deprived
horses. Our stables have been left for
children.

Thomas W. Shapcott

City Jungle

Here I am
In the jungle city.
Tigers, like cars
Chase our feet.
Wild birds,
Like children
Scream bitterly.
Elephants lumber around
Like buses,
Giraffes have necks
As tall as buildings
And the monkeys' chatter
Sounds like my sister's.

Nicole Townsend

shopping trolleys

notice how they have perfect steering
until you put something in them

their automatic response is to apply the brakes.
however they can be goaded forward

by the application of a foot sharply placed
on the rear bottom bar. surprise is essential.

you can make them move their wheels
but there is no guarantee that they will all move

in the same direction. the poor things
are terrified & only want to escape. an average

family shopping turns them into nervous
wrecks for weeks. you might think that those

trolleys you see out in carparks & under
sapling trees are sight-seeing. they aren't.

they're trying to avoid having things put in them.
it's hopeless. there's always someone who wants

to use them as garbage bins laundry baskets
billy carts or flower pots. or bassinettes.

they are prolific breeders in the wild
& run in enormous herds

they rust in captivity & frequently collapse
during use. recovery is unusual

Jenny Boult

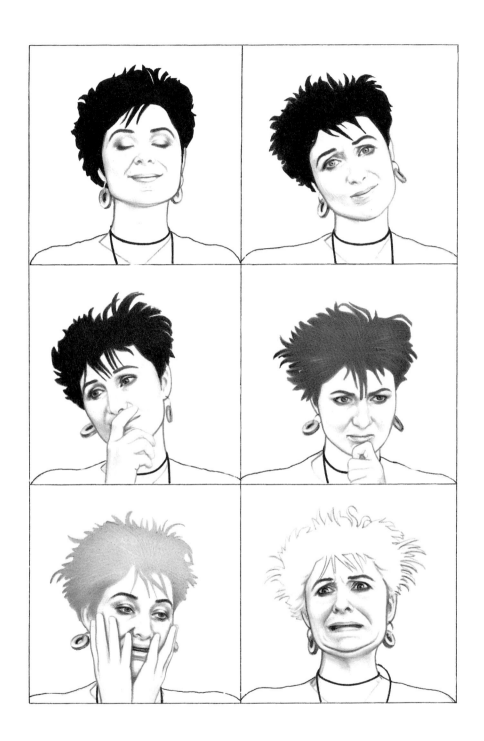

60

shopping

look over there in that window
isn't that lovely
the sort of thing that would
go with your hair
it would look nice on you

we'll go & try it on
shall we?
well, all right. perhaps not
a bit saggy in the neck

well. what about this one?
i've told you before
i haven't got money to throw away
on rubbish

i don't like that
you know that kind of thing
looks terrible with your shoulders

you don't want that.
that's not what we're looking for.
you've several of those already.

what about this?
in another colour?
if they have it in your size.

i won't throw money away.
i've told you. no. no. no.
definitely not.
i don't care who else is wearing them

i can't understand
why you're so difficult
to please

Jenny Boult

about auntie rose & her diet

my auntie rose says
"no sugar for me
just a little artificial sweetener
in my cup of tea"

she says
"just half a slice
of that lovely cake.
it looks so nice"

so she eats one half slice
& another half slice
& another half slice
& another
& another
& another

& her eyes glaze.
i can almost see her
growing fatter & fatter
till the cake's all gone & then
she says "oh well
it doesn't really matter
there's another one in the fridge
on a baked meringue platter"

when she's eaten that she laughs
she says "my clothes don't fit me
any more" & we're off on the bus
to the larger ladies' fashion store

after that she says "my word,
that's really worn me out
it must be lunchtime
my stomach's crying out for food"

in the coffee shop she says,
"i'm back on the diet
no sugar for me
just a little artificial sweetener
in my cup of tea

that dress i bought
is on the big side, so while we're here
let's have a pie
& half a slice of that lovely cake
it looks so nice . . ."

Jenny Boult

I can untangle lines

so
they think my brother's cute
just because he wears a pink singlet
and board shorts
that look like a mouldy fruit salad

and blonde hair that sticks up
and long brown legs
and goes to high school

I've got old footy shorts
a new fishing rod
a red plastic bucket
with cockles
and a rag
and a knife in it

and I can untangle lines
all by myself

Jo Chesher

my brother's voice is breaking

the languid day dwindles
into a heap of thin-ribbed clouds
lying lazily along a skyline
flushed with fever
soon it is dark
and the moon squints along the black road
shining on
mud
puddles
and a black shape
huddled in the gloom
lurking
behind the hedge
at the back gate
my brother angus

he is lying in wait for olive
the daughter of our milkman
she never speaks to him
but he likes to prowl
and watch
olive
sometimes he puffs at a cigarette
it makes him sick
but it impresses olive
he believes
angus is fifteen
father is having a good deal of trouble
with him
angus is having a good deal of trouble
with his voice
which is breaking

olive passes
angus watches
watches olive
then throws down his cigarette
his boot squashes it in the black mud
then he goes inside
tea is ready

Redmond Phillips

IV

Possums

We've possums in our roof—how very sweet!
You'd think I'd hear the patter of their feet.
You'd think I'd wake sometimes from peaceful sleep
Aroused by gentle rustling as they creep
On rafters in our spider-muffled loft.
You'd think I'd hear them scamper, velvet-soft,
These smoky shadows flitting overhead
With delicate and dainty-tripping tread.

Huh!

They thunder round the racetrack of the beams,
Then organise themselves in football teams;
Their games are much like ours are, on the whole—
I'll swear I've heard triumphant yells of "Goal!",
A frightful thud as two of them collide,
And uproar as they bellow out "Offside!"
Then scuffles, whacks and wallops as they fight—
A thumping possum rumpus in the night.

Ann Coleridge

Spiders

They can be big
They can be small
But I like any spiders at all.
I like spiders because they crawl.
    They can be thin
    They can be fat
    I like spiders because of that.
    I like spiders that live under the mat.
        They can be red
        They can be black
        But I like the ones with green on their back.
        I found one of these in the firewood stack.
            They can be round
            They can be square
            But I like the ones that can live anywhere
            AS LONG AS THEY DON'T TRY TO LAND IN MY HAIR.

                              Katharine Woffenden

The Famine and The Feast

Cackle and lay, cackle and lay!
How many eggs did you get today?
None in the manger, and none in the shed,
None in the box where the chickens are fed,
None in the tussocks and none in the tub,
And only a little one out in the scrub.
Oh I say! Dumplings today.
I fear that the hens must be laying away.

Cackle and lay, cackle and lay!
How many eggs did you get today?
Two in the manger and four in the shed,
Six in the box where the chickens are fed,
Two in the tussocks and ten in the tub,
And nearly two dozen right out in the scrub.
Hip, hooray! Pudding today!
I think the hens are beginning to lay.

C. J. Dennis

A New Ending for an Old Rhyme

One, two, three—
Mother caught a flea—
Put it in the teapot
And made a cup of tea.
Four, five, six—
The flea's in a fix—
Swimming in the water
And giving final kicks—
Seven, eight, nine,
The flea's doing fine!
We left him for the winter
And turned him into wine—
Get to ten—
And go back again
Ten back to one—
Wasn't that fun?

Sally Farrell Odgers

Tea

Making a cup of tea
Is like doing an easy sum
Like 13 + 14
Or 17 + 1.

Putting in the water
Milk and the tea
It's really very simple
It's easy see!

Josephine Moss

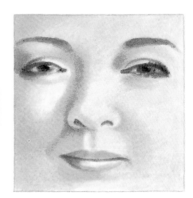

I Think I'm Going To

I've a fickle little tickle
In my nostril, if you please,
With an itching and a twitching—
I think I'm going to sneeze.

I've a squiggle of a giggle
In my throat, behind my scarf,
An immortal little chortle—
I think I'm going to laugh.

I'm so cosy, I'm so dozy,
I can keep awake no more,
I'm so weary and so bleary—
I think I'm going to . . .

Peter Wesley-Smith

From **K'shoo**

Whed your dose is code as barble,
   Ad you sduffle all the day,
Ad your head id is behavig
   Id a bost udbleased way;
Whed your ev'ry joid is achig
   With a very paidful cramb,
Whed your throad is dry ad tiglish,
   Ad your feed are code ad damb;
Whed your eyes are red ad rudding
   With the dears that will cub oud;
You cad safely bake your bind ub
   There is very liddle doubd.

You've got a code—a code—
   Ad idfluedzal code;
You cahd tell how you caughd id,
   But id's got a good firb hode.
Your face is whide, your eyes are pigk,
   Your dose is red ad blue;
Ad you wish that you were—
   Ah-Ah-Ah-h-Kish-SHOO-O-O!

               C. J. Dennis

Alas!

We've read of it in rhymes, alas!
We've seen it many times, alas!
    And bards have sung
    In every tongue
In warm and frigid climes, alas!

And everyone has read, alas!
The phrase that makes our head—alas!
    But never met
    A person yet
Who ever really *said* "Alas!"

W. T. Goodge

Be Nice To Rhubarb

Please say a word for rhubarb,
  It hasn't many chums
For people like banana splits
  Or fancy juicy plums.

They slice the sweet, sweet melon
  Or gather tasty pears,
But if you mention rhubarb pie
  You get the *rhu*dest stares.

They praise the yellow lemon,
  The golden orange cool,
But rhubarb's never mentioned
  —Or that's the general *rhu*le.

For rhubarb stewed and blushing
  I've only this to say,
If they should cast an unkind barb
  I'll see they *rhu* the day.

Max Fatchen

Puffer Fish

My sister had a puffer fish
She caught it from the pier
An oily, slimy puffer fish,
It lasted for a year.
And if you took it by surprise
Or frightened it or swore,
It puffed till it was twice the size
That it had been before.

Alas, one day the puffer fish
Completely disappeared
While puss looked rather devilish
With whiskers oily-smeared
And none of us believed our eyes
When suddenly we saw
Our puss puff up to twice the size
That she had been before.

Doug MacLeod

Sitting on the Fence

"Come sit down beside me,"
I said to myself,
And although it doesn't make sense,
I held my own hand
As a small sign of trust
And together I sat on the fence.

Michael Leunig

Jane

Jane built a fire truck
and now she's in disgrace.
Every fire that she put out
was in its fireplace.

Michael Dugan

Seafood

A sardine is thin and small
and combats hunger not at all,
a whale is large and rather stately
and fills one up quite adequately.

Michael Dugan

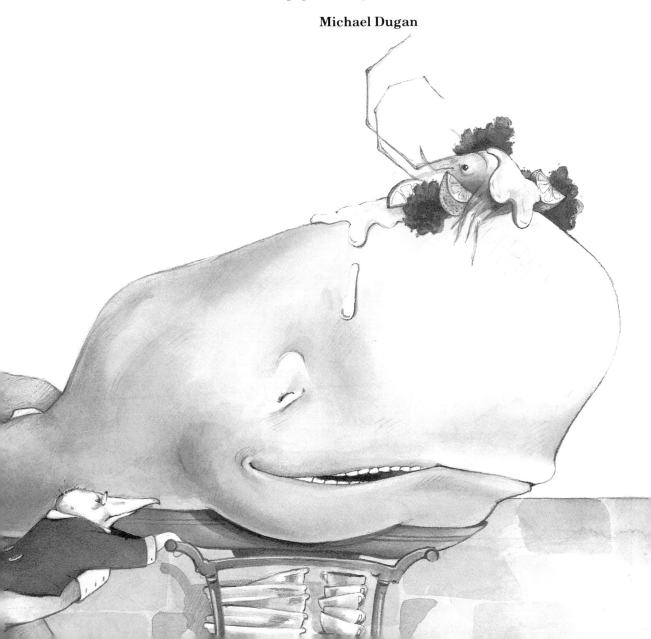

Bold Bruce Backward

Bruce Backward was an outlaw
His ways were bold and blunt
And everything that outlaws did
Bold Bruce did back-to-front.

He bailed up a coach and pair
One morning bright and sunny
Roared, "Everybody make a move!"
Then gave them all his money.

He burst into the local bank
With robbery in mind
Then, chuckling, he stole the safe
And left the gold behind.

His first attempt at kidnapping
Was backward as could be
The ransom note said "Pay up
Or I'll set the children free."

Alas, the law caught up with Bruce
They tried him in the street
And, since it was his last request,
They hanged him by the feet.

Doug MacLeod

Breakfast Ballad

"If there's anythin' better than lyin' on
    leaves,
  It's risin' from leaves at dawnin',
If there's anythin' better than sleepin'
    at eve,
  It's wakin' up in the mawnin'.

"If there's anythin' better than camp
    firelight,
  It's bright sunshine on wakin'.
If there's anythin' better than puddin'
    at night,
  It's puddin' when day is breakin'.

"If there's anythin' better than singin' away
  While the stars are gaily shinin',
Why, it's singin' a song at dawn of day,
  On puddin' for breakfast dinin'."

Norman Lindsay

Station Life

Oh, a station life is the life for me,
   And the cold baked mutton in the morning!
Oh, the glorious ride o'er the plains so free,
   And the cold baked mutton in the morning!
And the rising moon on the mountain's brow!
And the ringtailed possum on the gum tree bough!
And the leathery damper and the salted cow,
   And the cold baked mutton in the morning!

                           W. T. Goodge

Down the River

I've done with joys an' misery,
    An' why should I repine?
There's no one knows the past but me
    An' that ol' dog o' mine.
We camp, an' walk, an' camp, an' walk,
    An' find it fairly good;
He can do anything but talk—
    An' wouldn't, if he could.

We sits an' thinks beside the fire,
    With all the stars ashine,
An' no one knows our thoughts but me
    An' that there dog o' mine.
We has our Johnny-cake an' scrag,
    An' finds 'em fairly good;
He can do anything but talk—
    An' wouldn't, if he could.

Henry Lawson

Daley's Dorg Wattle

"You can talk about yer sheep dorgs," said the man from
Allan's Creek,
"But I know a dorg that simply knocked 'em bandy!
Do whatever you would show him, and you'd hardly need
to speak.
Owned by Daley, drover cove in Jackandandy.

"We was talkin' in the parlour, me and Daley, quiet like,
When a blowfly starts a-buzzin' round the ceilin',
Up gets Daley, and he says to me, "You wait a minute,
Mike.
And I'll show you what a dorg he is at heelin'.'"

"And an empty pickle-bottle was a-standin' on the shelf,
Daley takes it down and puts it on the table,
And he bets me drinks that blinded dorg would do it by
himself—
And I didn't think as how as he was able!

"Well, he shows the dorg the bottle, and he points up to the
fly,
And he shuts the door, and says to him—"Now Wattle!"
And in less than fifteen seconds, spare me days, it ain't a
lie,
That there dorg had got that inseck in the bottle!"

W. T. Goodge

The Crocodile Overlanders

No doubt you've heard of droving trips across the barren
dry,
And how they brought the bullocks down in the good old
days gone by;
But the greatest droving episode that any man has made
Was thirty thousand crocodiles, from the Gulf to Adelaide.

I've never seen the likes of them, this mob of crocodiles,
Thirty-footers, every one, strung out for thirty miles,
It took three days to start them off, three days to
straighten up,
Three days we'd travel southward then three days to block
'em up.

They had abnormal appetites, as any lizard should,
Anything with hair and hide was considered very good.
The first day out from Normanton we lost the jackaroo
Then, blow me down the horses went, and the old blue
heeler too!

The last we saw of Goanna Bob, our horse-tailer of repute,
He was headed towards the rabbit-proof with a big croc in
pursuit.
While drifting down the Flinders they cracked on a bit of
pace,
They met a mob of bullocks, and they never left a trace!

They were long and lean and cranky, they had teeth like
crosscut saws,
And, travelling through the timber, just to exercise their
jaws
They churned out hardwood posts, one foot six by seven
tall,
And left them by the stock route, all barked and sapped
and all.

88

By spinifex and saltbush plains and along the old Georgina
They snapped and snarled and fought for they were slowly
getting meaner.
They didn't like the spinifex a-tickling their hides,
And with water getting far apart, the tears came to their
eyes.

You've heard of crocodile tears, but look! you wouldn't
know the meaning!
With thirty thousand shedding tears, (and seeing was
believing!)
There was water in the gullies, there was water in the
creeks
And the old Georgina River running belly-deep for weeks!

It proved our great salvation, for on that flood of tears
We sailed them straight past Lake Eyre on the biggest
flood for years.
A short step then to Adelaide, and delivery right on time,
For the agent came to meet us, and here's the ending to
this rhyme,

He said, "You'll have to turn them round and take them
back again!
The fashion now for ladies' shoes is imitation crocodile,
And it's got a coarser grain!"

Tom Oliver

Tall Timber

Just south of the Murray where tall timbers grow,
I saw seven gum trees all set in a row,
And their tips were so high they were covered in snow.

Tall timber! Tall timber!
The tall timber grows where the big rivers are,
But the yarns that they tell you are taller by far.

I said to an old bloke, Say those trees are tall,
But he said to me, Brother, you're right off the ball,
Those mean little saplings they aren't trees at all.

If you're talking of timber, the old fellow said,
I was once driving bullocks, when whoa, strike me dead,
I looked up and there was the river ahead.

I just stood there cursing, my feet in the mud;
The sight was enough to have frozen your blood,
The river a mile wide was raging in flood.

But a dead gum was growing a furlong away,
So I out with my axe, and it took me a day,
But I cut the cow down and it fell the right way.

And it stretched several miles to the land past the tide,
So I called to my bullocks, "Up there, blast your hide!"
And we crossed the big flood through the gum tree's inside.

But wait, I must tell you, at close of the day,
We were still in the tree when we heard a loud "Hey!"
From a bullock team coming the opposite way.

It was coming head on, we were set for a smash,
And I thought for a moment we just had to crash,
But I swung on my whip and I gave 'em the lash.

And I cursed, and I swore, and I sang 'em a hymn,
And though in that trunk it was murky and dim,
I could see branching leftwards a small hollow limb.

So I drove my beasts down it, we found our way through,
And we came out near Sydney in Woolloomooloo,
And as sure as I'm sober this story is true.

Tall timber! Tall timber!
The tall timber grows where the big rivers are,
But the yarns that they tell you are taller by far.

Len Fox

The Old Man's Song

When I was a young man, I followed the gold,
Deep in a mineshaft, all muddy and cold.
Deep in the dark with a flickering light
And never a nugget to gladden my sight—
But it's way, hey! Now I am old,
The mornings were silver, the sunsets were gold.

When I was a young man, I followed the sea.
Cold, wet and shivering often I'd be;
Rocked in the crow's nest or rolled down below
Or sweating my soul out where the Gulf traders go—
But it's way, hey! Now I am old,
The oceans were sapphires, the beaches were gold.

Now I am an old man, I sit in the sun;
Thinking and dreaming of things that I've done.
Remembering laughter, forgetting the pain
And I'd go out and do it all over again—
Way, hey! Lift it along!
What good is your life if it isn't a song?

Bill Scott

93

V

Island Song

I rode my horse through the singing bush
In the green month
In the gold month
September soft on the island:
When the scented wattle blows
And the red heath glows
And Spring comes laughing to the island.

I rode my horse through the breathless bush
In the sunbright month
In the shimmer month
February flame on the island:
When the bark lies firecrack dry
As the lonely snake slides by
O, Summer has two faces on the island!

I rode my horse through the whispering bush
In the mistgrey month
In the dreaming month
May smiling warm on the island:
Cobwebs cluster like phantom flowers
Currawong calls from the gums' high towers
Autumn lingering late on the island.

I rode my horse through the rain-sad bush
In the dark month
In the black month
July creeping slow on the island:
Frost firming the shadowed trail
Keen and southerly blows the gale
Winter storming over the island.

Betty Roberts

Graveyard Creek

At the bottom of the paddock
a creek runs from the hills,
a stream of water that carries legends
and shadows from the past—
that eagles soar above majestically
and the Lion's Head Range stares down upon.

Local farmers tell of Aboriginal tribes
that lived below Mount Warning
and vanished after the settlement of white men—
leaving their middens
on the banks of this creek
and the edge of huge cedar forests.

A tangle of vines and ferns
crowds together in dense clusters
as if guarding an ancient secret—
above the transparent shroud of water
that reveals brown patterns
of twigs and whitened pebbles.

Below spires of silky oaks,
wild strawberries and thistles
throw up splashes of colour
to attract a stranger's attention—
or a rainbow-bird, poised in flight,
flashes past to its sandy hollow.

The vast silence of mountains
flows past in that water
as it trickles and swirls in brief shallows—
broken only by the voice of the breeze
that whispers like a ghost
as it drifts through evergreen shadows.

Peter Skrzynecki

Egrets

Once as I travelled through a quiet evening,
I saw a pool, jet-black and mirror-still.
Beyond, the slender paperbarks stood crowding;
each on its own white image looked its fill,
and nothing moved but thirty egrets wading—
thirty egrets in a quiet evening.

Once in a lifetime, lovely past believing,
your lucky eyes may light on such a pool.
As though for many years I had been waiting,
I watched in silence, till my heart was full
of clear dark water, and white trees unmoving,
and, whiter yet, those thirty egrets wading.

Judith Wright

Ringneck Parrots

Translated by T. G. H. Strehlow

The ringneck parrots, in scattered flocks,
The ringneck parrots are screaming in their upward flight.

The ringneck parrots are a cloud of wings;
The shell parrots are a cloud of wings.

Let the shell parrots come down to rest,
Let them come down to rest on the ground!

Let the caps fly off the scented blossoms!
Let the blooms descend to the ground in a shower!

The clustering bloodwood blooms are falling down,
The clustering bloodwood blossoms, nipped by birds.

The clustering bloodwood blooms are falling down,
The clustering bloodwood blossoms, one by one.

Aboriginal: Aranda

Thunderstorm

Nearly every afternoon that summer
a thunderstorm broke
like a battle in the sky—
where heroes and villains
clashed in combat and hurled down
their clamour of deafening cries.

First the wind, then the thunder;
then lightning that split
huge clouds apart—
then jagged hailstones
and rain like nails
that ripped open the forest
and tore up the shelters in tufts of grass.

Birds grew silent.
Cows and horses herded themselves
under willows and pines.
Dogs hid under the house.
Chickens left the yard.

We stayed like prisoners in the house
and watched the tumult
wash against our castle of weatherboard
and corrugated iron—
                              pressing our faces
against the glass—
and heard the fear in each other's heart.

Afterwards we walked
like heroes ourselves, barefooted,
through paddocks strewn with leaves and ice—
threw handfuls of it
into the sky like diamonds
and pretended we hadn't been afraid.

A rainbow would form
over the land
and hang like a magic charm—

and we believed
as long as it always appeared
nothing bad would ever happen to the farm.

Peter Skrzynecki

Rainwater Tank

Empty rings when tapped give tongue,
rings that are tense with water talk:
as he sounds them, ring by rung,
Joe Mitchell's reddened knuckles walk.

The cattledog's head sinks down a notch
and another notch, beside the tank,
and Mitchell's boy, with an old jack-plane,
lifts moustaches from a plank.

From the puddle that the tank has dripped
hens peck glimmerings and uptilt
their heads to shape the quickness down;
petunias live on what gets spilt.

The tankstand spider adds a spittle
thread to her portrait of her soul.
Pencil-grey and stacked like shillings
out of a banker's paper roll

stands the tank, roof-water drinker.
The downpipe stares drought into it.
Briefly the kitchen tap turns on
then off. But the tank says Debit, Debit.

Les A. Murray

Driving North

I am now north of the city
two hundred miles or more away,
and regret already the green
I have left behind. This plain
my great-grandparents walked into
and my parents out of, hopelessly.
It is bright and bony and dry,
the dust dances and dances, alive
as snakes, and the paddocks spread
and burn like beer bottle glass.
There can be no rational tears
for a land like this, but I
am misty-eyed for a distant boy
who could climb the lonely trees,
who watched the glass-bright sky
for cloud, who counted the years
between the flash and the thunder,
and sometimes sang in the brief rain.

John Griffin

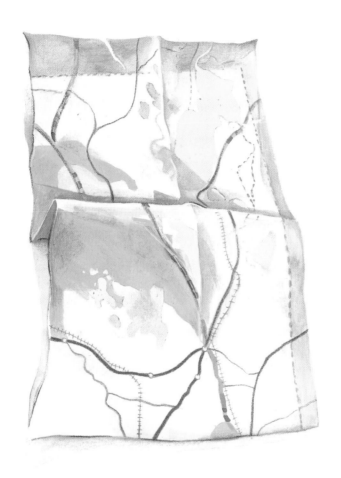

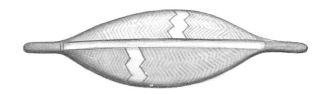

Bwalla the Hunter

In the hard famine time, in the long drought
Bwalla the hunter on walkabout,
Lubra and children following slow,
All proper hungry long time now.

No more kangaroo out on the plain,
Gone to other country where there was rain.
Couldn't find emu, couldn't find seed,
And the children all time cry for feed.

They saw great eagle come through the sky
To his big stick gunya in a gum near by,
Fine young wallaby carried in his feet:
He bring tucker for his kids to eat.

Big fella eagle circled slow,
Little fella eagles fed below.
"Gwa!" said Bwalla the hunter, "he
Best fella hunter, better than me."

He dropped his boomerang. "Now I climb,
All share tucker in the hungry time.
We got younks too, we got need—
You make fire and we all have feed."

Then up went Bwalla like a native cat,
All the blackfellows climb like that.
And when he look over big nest rim
Those young ones all sing out at him.

They flapped and spat, they snapped and clawed,
They plenty wild with him, my word,
They shrilled at tucker-thief big and brown,
But Bwalla took wallaby and then climbed down.

Kath Walker

108

The Food Gatherers

We are the food gatherers, we
And all the busy lives we see,
Fur and feathers, the large and small,
With Nature's plenty for us all:
The hawk circling over the plains,
The dingo, scourge of his domains,
The lone owl whose voice forlorn
Pursues the sunset into dawn.
Even the small bronze chickowee
That gossips in bright melody—
Look, into the clump he's gone,
He has a little murder on!
For food is life and life is still
The old carnage, and all must kill
Others, though why wise Nature planned
Red rapine, who can understand?
Only for food, never for sport,
That new evil the white man brought.
Lovely to see them day by day,
The food gatherers, busy and gay,
But most of all we love our own,
When as the dulled red sun goes down
Fishers and hunters home return
To where the family fires burn.
Food now and merriment,
Bellies full and all content,
Around the fires at wide nightfall,
This the happiest time of all.

Kath Walker

Place Names

Ethadinna, Mira Mitta,
Mulka, Mungerannie—
Dark shadows blown
With the dust away,
Far from our day
Far out of time,
Fill the land with water.
Where the blue sky flames
On the bare red stone,
Dulkaninna, Koperamanna,
Ooroowilanie, Kilalpaninna—
Only the names
In the land remain
Like a dark well
Like the chime of a bell.

Douglas Stewart

"Where's Schell?"

for Alma McMahon

He certainly detested George Schell's dog.
The words "where's Schell" would catapult him round
the tankstand. Hedgehog-hackled, thyroid-eyed
he'd rumble there, ears sifting wind for sounds
of George's Chev-four truck that clattered by
on wheezing, steamed excursions into town.

Gates shuddered as he raced towards the road
and as he rasped beneath the bottom rails
he left a fringe of chocolate-coloured hair
along the splintered wood. His bellow trailed
his progress like a shadow pausing where
he scraped against the ring-lock-netting nails.

And so the Chev-led tumult trundled on.
While Schell pawed roaring circles round the tray
Choc barked his hakas from the dust that flowed
around their bawling progress storeward. Waves
of foamed invective faded as George towed
his raucous dustcloud slowly through the haze.

He'd lumber homeward from his mobile war
parched barkless and his back the balder from
one more encounter with the netting-gates.
Back underneath the tankstand he'd lie prone,
eyes beaded roadward, swivel-eared, and wait
for sounds of George's rattling journey home.

When I returned last year I ran my hand
along a weathered slab of yellow box
that forms a bottom rail. The hair had gone.
But then so had the house and George and Choc—
these forty years and more. One gate alone
remains and rattles in its rusted lock.

But now it's just the wind.

Frank McMahon

Windmill

The windmill by the water tank
with its see-through face
and base
of latticed iron bars
has become a fisherman
standing in the shallows
of a lake full of minnows
featureless horizon to horizon

who suddenly enmeshes the water
with a throwing-net of galahs.

William Hart-Smith

Stump Picking

Out after mallee roots,
erect as mine prongs
across the paddocks.
Alive and deadly,
ticking with beetles.

Behind our backs
tusks and horns
rear up from the earth,
lumpy rhinoceros
menacing the ploughlands.

If they were stones
we could build a barn,
a house, a wall—
with mid-day hunger
we stacked the truck
with caves full of air.

Unloading at night,
aim for the heap—
bobbing in the darkness
by the light of our lantern
Storing up warmth and firelight.

Christine Churches

Easterly

for Amy

Windmills face the way it came from.
Dustclouds stream
from backs of tractors. Dried-out thistles
crackle in the paddocks. Tussocks lean
on western fences. Pepper boughs sweep dirt in circles.
Box thorns whistle
high on hillsides. Wind clouds glide
through scoured-out sky-light. Creek beds wither.
Ibis hide.
Fennel bends.
Reeds blow dry.

Chaff shed rafters shelter sparrows.
Fowls stay home.
Kelpies curl on folded wheatbags. Seed pods blown
from thistles catch in cobwebs or
collect in corners. Harness swings
on stable doors.

Generators sway and rattle.
Guy-wires strain.
Racing vanes spin light to read by. Evening sounds
creep in through curtains. Locking chains
send haunting noises round verandahs.
Smoke blows down
in kitchen chimneys. As it goes
wind tops the tanks up. Pump rods rumble.
Water flows.
Stock-troughs ripple.
Cannas grow.

Frank McMahon

VI

They Knew

—the answers to important questions—why
cats peer at kitchen fires, sly-eyed
through gaps in grates—why kelpies sleep
on chaff bags, curled in circles—how they keep
their feet on tossing truck-trays when they ride
by squinting at the wind—why tin roofs creak
and crackle when the winter frosts begin

—why sleeping fowls pawk softly in the night
—why pressure lanterns hiss—why light
they cast greens shadows when it arcs
in circles on the ceilings and the dark
backs off to crouch in corners—why the flights
of teal form vees in evenings—why the marsh
gleams eerily when river mists creep in

—why stones are placed on gate-posts—why they hung
the lantern by the landing—why the gums
have boat-shaped bark scars where they line
the river by the island. Now I find
that I've left the answers somewhere there among
the faces in a place where there was time
and reasons in the world and answers when

I needed them. Forgotten now; although
there's little missed—there's no one here who knows
the questions now.

Frank McMahon

Dream of a Bird

You ask me, what did I dream?
I dreamt I became a bird.
You ask me, why did I want to become a bird?
I really wanted to have wings.
You ask me, why did I want wings?
These wings would help me fly back to my country.
You ask me, why did I want to go back there?
Because I wanted to find something I missed.
You ask me, what do I miss?
I miss the place where I lived as a child.
You ask me, what was that place like?
That place was happy, my family was close together.
You ask me, what I remember best?
I still remember, my father reading the newspaper.
You ask me, why I think of him?
I miss him and I'm sad.
You ask me, why I am sad?
I'm sad because all my friends have fathers.
You ask me, why does this matter?
Because my father is far away.
I want to fly to him like a bird.

Bach Nga Thi Tran

Coorong

Sweet bitter memories of yester years,
Smart my eyes with sudden tears,
I didn't know then it never could last,
That I'd look back and it would be past.

Preserved in love and stored in my heart,
Of travelling the Coorong in Uncle's old cart,
Setting up camp in just the right corner,
Gathering firewood to make us all warmer.

The kids catching fish and yabbies around,
Or digging for yams in the sweet-smelling ground,
Duck, prickly pears, swan eggs by the dozen,
Made each day a picnic for me and my cousins.

Syrup on damper and sweet billy tea,
They're planted forever in my memory,
Sitting by the fire when the night grew cold,
Hanging on to each word of the tales being told.

Hymns hummed at first then bursting to singing,
Our music top note set the old Coorong ringing,
Hunting and climbing and swimming all day,
How could we guess it would soon slip away?

Everything changing, the years gone so fast,
Only the Coorong standing steadfast,
Sharing with everyone over the years,
Memories laced with bitter-sweet tears.

Margaret Brusnahan

Captain Cook

Related by Percy Mumbulla

Tungeei, that was her native name.
She was a terrible tall woman
who lived at Ulladulla.
She had six husbands,
an' buried the lot.

She was over a hundred, easy,
when she died.
She was tellin' my father,
they were sittin' on the point
that was all wild scrub.

The big ship came and anchored
out at Snapper Island.
He put down a boat
an' rowed up the river
into Bateman's Bay.

He landed on the shore of the river,
the other side from where the
church is now.
When he landed he gave the Kurris clothes,
an' those big sea-biscuits.
Terrible hard biscuits they was.

When they were pullin' away to go back
to the ship, these wild Kurris
were runnin' out of the scrub.
They'd stripped right off again.
They were throwin' the clothes an' biscuits
back at Captain Cook
as his men were pullin' away in the boat.

Roland Robinson

Inside

Coming from the wilytjas,
from the camps, from the campfires,
coming at the string-end of an afternoon—
barefoot, up the steps, standing on the porch,
faces pressed against the fly-wire door:
   "We want inside! We want inside!"
Coming for oranges, coming for cool drinks,
coming for anything—for photos:
   "Pitjur! Pitjur! We bin laugh!"

   "We want inside! We want inside!"

Arms around each other's necks,
hair, sticking out in all directions—
brown at the roots,
   blonde at the tips
(the kind of style that costs
fifty bucks in the city).
Dresses hanging like empty flour sacks.

   "We want inside! We want inside!"

Kangaroo breath on their skin,
scars on the legs from boils and hot embers,
one or two bung-eyes in the group,
runny noses . . . children:
Norma and Jeannie sharing a lizard,
holding it up like a ticket:
small admission to linoleum
and electric fan.

Billy Marshall-Stoneking

Spirit Belong Mother

I not see you long time now, I not see you long time now,
White fella bin take me from you, I don't know why
Give me to missionary to be God's child
Give me new language, give me new name
All time I cry, they say — that shame
I go to city down south, real cold
I forget all your stories, my mother you told
Gone is my spirit, my dreaming, my name
Gone to these people, our country to claim
They gave me white mother, she give me new name
All time I cry, she say — that shame,
I not see you long time now, I not see you long time now.

I grow as woman now, not piccaninny no more
I need you to teach me your wisdom, your lore
I am your spirit, I'll stay alive
But in white fella way, you won't survive
I'll fight for your land, for your sacred sites
To sing and to dance with the brolga in flight
To continue to live in your own tradition —
A culture for me was replaced by a mission
I not see you long time now, I not see you long time now.

One day your dancing your dreaming your song
Will take me your spirit back where I belong
My mother the earth, the land, I demand
Protection from aliens who rule, who command
For they do not know where our dreaming began
Our destiny lies in the laws of white man
Two women we stand, our story untold
But now as our spiritual bondage unfold
We will silence this burden, this longing, this pain
When I hear you my mother, give me my name
I not see you long time now, I not see you long time now.

Eva Johnson

Wood Choppers

Chop the wood my children,
Your grandma's going to rest.
Then tie it in a bundle
To put upon my back.

Chop, chop went the shiny blade,
Throwing out the chips
As we swung our arms in rhythm,
Up and down upon the sticks.

Our grandma sat and watched us
As we carried to and fro,
And told us of her childhood
While we tied the bundles so.

While slowly walking homeward
Along the dusty track,
She'd often stop to shift the
Load of sticks upon her back.

And following close behind her
With pride in every step,
We walked just like our grandma
With our bundles on our backs.

Leila Rankine

Dawn Wail for the Dead

Dim light of daybreak now
Faintly over the sleeping camp.
Old lubra first to wake remembers:
First thing every dawn
Remember the dead, cry for them.
Softly at first her wail begins,
One by one as they wake and hear,
Join in the cry, and the whole camp
Wails for the dead, the poor dead
Gone from here to the Dark Place:
They are remembered.
Then it is over, life now,
Fires lit, laughter now,
And a new day calling.

Kath Walker

This earth . . .
I never damage,
I look after.
Fire is nothing,
just clean up.
When you burn,
New grass coming up.
That mean good animal soon . . .
might be goose, long-neck turtle, goanna, possum.
Burn him off . . .
new grass coming up,
new life all over.

Bill Neidjie

Index of Authors

Index of Poem Titles

Index of First Lines

Acknowledgments

Bateson, David: "Kim's Collection" published in *Education*. Permission: David Bateson.

Beach, Eric: "bird hits boy" © Eric Beach. Permission: Eric Beach.

Bell, Anne: "Milking Song" published in *Verse in Australia 1960* (Australian Letters). Permission: Anne Bell.

Boult, Jenny: "the school lunch poem", "where are you going?", "shopping", "shopping trolleys" and "about auntie rose & her diet" © Jenny Boult. Permission: Jenny Boult.

Brusnahan, Margaret: "Coorong" © Margaret Brusnahan. Permission: Margaret Brusnahan.

Campbell, David: "Snail" published in *Makar* (Queensland University) 1978. Permission: Curtis Brown (Aust) Pty Ltd.

Chesher, Jo: "I can untangle lines" © Jo Chesher. Permission: Jo Chesher.

Churches, Christine: "Stump Picking" published in *Dots Over Lines* edited by Graham Rowlands (A.U. Union Press) 1980. Permission: Christine Churches.

Coleridge, Ann: "Possums" © Ann Coleridge. Permission: Ann Coleridge.

Dennis, C. J.: "The Famine", "The Feast", from *A Book for Kids* by C. J. Dennis © Angus & Robertson Publishers 1921; extract from "K'shoo" from *Backblock Ballads & Later Verses* by C. J. Dennis © Angus & Robertson Publishers 1918. Permission: Angus & Robertson Publishers.

Dugan, Michael: "Macartney's Cow" published in *The Age*; "Bamboo Tiger" published in *Missing People* by Michael Dugan (Sweeney Reed Publications) 1970; "Seafood", "Jane", © Michael Dugan. Permission: Michael Dugan.

Fatchen, Max: "Tide Talk", "Down and Up", "Children Lost" © Max Fatchen. Permission: John Johnson Authors' Agent Ltd. "Be Nice to Rhubarb" from *Songs For My Dog and other people* by Max Fatchen (Kestrel Books) 1980, © 1980 Max Fatchen. Permission: Penguin Books Ltd.

Fox, Len: "Tall Timber", © Len Fox. Permission: Len Fox.

Griffin, John: "Driving North" published in *The Australian*. Permission: John Griffin.

Guess, Jeff: "Watermelons" published in *Patterns* (Fremantle Arts Centre) 1985. Permission: Jeff Guess.

Hart-Smith, William: "Limpets" published in *Poems of Discovery* (Angus & Robertson) 1959 © William Hart-Smith 1959; "Windmill" published in *Australian Poetry 1970* (Angus & Robertson) 1970 © William Hart-Smith 1970. Permission: Angus & Robertson Publishers.

Johnson, Eva: "Spirit Belong Mother" © Eva Johnson. Permission: Eva Johnson.

Kipping, Adèle: "Fanfare" © Adèle Kipping. Permission: Adèle Kipping.

Knowles, Lee: "The Back Step" published in *School Paper* (Education Department of WA). Permission: Education Department of WA.

Lindsay, Norman: "Breakfast Ballad" from *The Magic Pudding* (Angus & Robertson Publishers) © Janet Glad 1970. Permission: Angus & Robertson Publishers.

MacLeod, Doug: "Puffer Fish", "Bold Bruce Backward" © Doug MacLeod. Permission: Doug MacLeod.

McMahon, Frank: "Where's Schell?", "Easterly", "They Knew" © Frank McMahon. Permission: Frank McMahon.

McMaster, Rhyll: "Back Steps Lookout" published in *Washing the Money* (Angus & Robertson) © Rhyll McMaster 1986. Permission: Angus & Robertson Publishers.

Marshall-Stoneking, Billy: "Inside" published in *Westerly* (University of WA) 1984. Permission: Billy Marshall-Stoneking.

Moss, Josephine: "Tea" © Josephine Moss. Permission: Josephine Moss.

Murray, Les A.: "Rainwater Tank" from *The Vernacular Republic Poems 1961–1981* (Angus & Robertson Publishers) © Les A. Murray 1982. Permission: Angus & Robertson Publishers.

Norman, Lilith: "The Sea" published in *School Magazine* (NSW Department of Education). Permission: Lilith Norman.

Odgers, Sally Farrell: "A New Ending for an Old Rhyme" © Sally Farrell Odgers. Permission: Sally Farrell Odgers.

Paech, Neil: Untitled poem, © Neil Paech. Permission: Neil Paech.

Pearson, K. F.: "Seashell" from *Messages of Things* (Friendly Street Poets) 1984 by K. F. Pearson. Permission: K. F. Pearson.

Phillips, Redmond: "all day sucker", "i can read upside down", "my brother's voice is breaking" from *Playing With Girls* (Reed & Harris) 1945 by Julian Prang. Permission: Redmond Phillips.

Rankine, Leila: "Wood Choppers" © Leila Rankine. Permission: Leila Rankine.

Roberts, Betty; "Island Song" published in *Poetry Australia*. Permission: Betty Roberts.

Robinson, Roland: "Captain Cook" published in *Altjeringa* (A.W. & A.H. Reed) 1970 by Roland Robinson. Permission: Roland Robinson.

Scott, Bill: "Frogs", "The Old Man's Song" © W. N. Scott. Permission: W. N. Scott.

Shapcott, Thomas W.: "Horses" published *LiNQ* (James Cook University) 1981. Permission: Thomas W. Shapcott.

Simpson, R. A.: "Lake" from *Diver* (University of Queensland Press) 1972 by R. A. Simpson. Permission: University of Queensland Press.

Skrzynecki, Peter: "Graveyard Creek", "Thunderstorm" © Peter Skrzynecki. Permission: Peter Skrzynecki.

Smith, Darien: "Sunstruck" first published in *Puffinalia* (Australian Puffin Club) 1980. Permission: Darien Smith.

Stewart, Douglas: "Place Names" from *Collected Poems 1936–1967* (Angus & Robertson) 1967 by Douglas Stewart, © Margaret Stewart 1967. Permission: Angus & Robertson Publishers.

Stow, Randolph: "A Wind from the Sea" from *Poetry Magazine*, 1964. Permission: Richard Scott Simon Ltd.

Talbot, Norman: "Plumpoem" published in *Poetry Australia*. Permission: Norman Talbot.

Tran, Bach Nga Thi: "Dream of a Bird" published in *Mosaic* (Findon High School, Adelaide). Permission: Bach Nga Thi Tran.

Walker, Kath: "Bwalla the Hunter", "The Food Gatherers", "Dawn Wail for the Dead" from *My People* (Jacaranda Wiley Ltd) 1970 by Kath Walker. Permission: Jacaranda Wiley Ltd.

Wallace-Crabbe, Chris: "Genius Loci" published in *The Age*. Permission: Chris Wallace-Crabbe.

Wardleworth, Samuel: "Cow Cocky" © Samuel Wardleworth. Permission: Samuel Wardleworth.

Wcarry, Catherine: Untitled poem, "Prawning" © Catherine Warry. Permission: Catherine Warry.

Wesley-Smith, Peter: "Short Song", "I Think I'm Going To" © Peter Wesley-Smith. Permission: Peter Wesley-Smith.

Wright, John: "Baggin'" published in *Westerly* (University of WA) 1980. Permission: John Wright.

Wright, Judith: "Night Herons", "Egrets" from *Collected Poems 1942–1970* (Angus & Robertson) © Judith Wright 1971. Permission: Angus & Robertson Publishers.